The
Perfect
Sale

THE PERFECT SERIES

ALL YOU NEED TO GET IT RIGHT FIRST TIME

OTHER TITLES IN THE SERIES:

The Perfect Appraisal by Howard Hudson

The Perfect Business Plan by Ron Johnson

Perfect Business Writing by Peter Bartram

The Perfect Career by Max Eggert

Perfect Communications by Andrew Leigh and Michael Maynard

The Perfect Conference by Iain Maitland

Perfect Customer Care by Ted Johns

The Perfect CV by Max Eggert

Perfect Decisions by Andrew Leigh

The Perfect Dismissal by John McManus

Perfect Financial Ratios by Terry Gasking

The Perfect Interview by Max Eggert

The Perfect Meeting by David Sharman

The Perfect Negotiation by Gavin Kennedy

The Perfect Presentation by Andrew Leigh and Michael Maynard

Perfect Recruitment by David Oates and Viv Shackleton

The Perfect Report by Peter Bartram

Perfect Stress Control by Carole McKenzie

Perfect Time Management by Ted Johns

The Perfect Sale

ALL YOU NEED
TO GET IT RIGHT
FIRST TIME

NICK THORNELY
and DAN LEES

ARROW
BUSINESS BOOKS

Published by Arrow Books in 1994

1 3 5 7 9 10 8 6 4 2

Nick Thornely and Dan Lees 1994

Nick Thornely and Dan Lees have asserted their rights under the
Copyright, Designs and Patents Act, 1988 to be identified as the
authors of this work.

First published by
Arrow Books Limited
20 Vauxhall Bridge Road, London SW1V 2SA

Random House Australia (Pty) Limited
20 Alfred Street, Milsons Point, Sydney
New South Wales 2061, Australia

Random House New Zealand Limited
18 Poland Road, Glenfield
Auckland 10, New Zealand

Random House South Africa (Pty) Limited
PO Box 337, Bergvlei, South Africa

Set in Bembo by
SX Composing Ltd., Rayleigh, Essex
Printed and bound in Great Britain by
Cox and Wyman Ltd, Reading, Berks

British Library Cataloguing in Publication Data
A catalogue record for this book is available from
the British Library

Random House UK Limited Reg. No. 954009
ISBN 0–09–937931–7

ABOUT THE AUTHORS

NICK THORNELY has had a long career in selling, much of it at board room level. He is Chairman of IML Employee Involvement Ltd, a leading consultancy specializing in employee involvement and motivation for organizations of all sizes.

DAN LEES is a journalist, broadcaster and author of more than 20 books. He learned his selling the hard way as salesman and sales manager and now sells mainly ideas, projects and, of course, himself.

CONTENTS

Introduction   ix

1. The Perfect Company   1

2. The Perfect Product   5

3. The Perfect Salesperson   8

4. Perfect Organization   12

5. The Perfect Customer   16

6. Motivating the Perfect Sale   20

7. The Perfectly Motivated Customer   25

8. Perfect Research   30

9. The Perfect Approach   34

10. The Perfect First Impression   39

11. The Perfect Presentation   46

12. The Perfect Demonstration   51

13. The Perfect Way to Handle Objections   56

14. The Perfect Close   61

15. The Perfect Exit   66

16. Perfect Records   70

17. Perfect SOBs and other challenges   74

18. Perfect Ways to Break the Mould   78

19. Perfect Business-Building   83

INTRODUCTION

Allow us to sell you the perfect sale.

If you are a professional salesperson, or wish to become one, aiming for perfect sales will help feed you and your family, provide lasting satisfaction for you and for your customers, maintain your company in business, increase its good name and keep its people employed.

If that is enough to arouse your *interest* in the concept, we can go on to solicit your *involvement* and to persuade you to *invest* a certain amount of time and effort.

In fact, the investment of time and effort is returnable, as quality selling will eventually save both.

All you need do is put into practice any of the suggestions in the book which make sense in your particular situation, even if some of them seem to be merely common sense.

QUALITY SELLING MEANS QUANTITY SALES

- Quality goods and services are easier to sell. (Your sales increase.)
- Selling the prospect a product which will fulfil THEIR needs and solve problems which THEY have identified makes for a perfect close. (Your sales increase.)
- Putting the prospect and their needs FIRST not only makes for rock–steady original orders but can lead to repeats and referrals. (Your sales increase.)
- After a perfect sale the prospect will have become not just a purchaser but a CUSTOMER, ie one who *customarily* buys from you. (Your sales increase.)

- Because the perfect sale involves the buyer in an ongoing long-term process, the customer becomesan enthusiastic advocate of your company and your product. (Your sales increase.)
- Aiming for perfect sales means that you feel better about your role as a PROFESSIONAL. You are confident and optimistic. (Your sales increase.)

As well as satisfying one of your major needs, by enabling you to produce more business, aiming for perfect sales will yield many other important satisfactions.

If all this sells you on the idea of aiming for perfect sales, you now need to consider those factors of the selling process which you can CONTROL and INFLUENCE – the first of which is the choice of your PERFECT COMPANY.

THE PERFECT COMPANY

In sales, perhaps more than in most professions, a man is known by the company that keeps him.

This means that the perfect sale begins when you start looking for a sales job with a company which will be the perfect company – FOR YOU.

You could already be in a sales position, or you could be a beginner whose choice is limited by lack of experience or the state of the economy. However, the company you work for remains a factor which sooner or later you can control or influence. Keep or take the best job you can get but, if the company is not perfect for you, carry on looking.

When looking for a company which will enable you to make perfect sales there are some factors which must be present whatever the organization or its product.

WHAT MAKES A PERFECT COMPANY?

To identify your perfect company, ask yourself if you would buy the firm if you were in a position to do so. This helps answer the question of whether it's the right company for you.

Ask yourself:

- has the company got a GOOD REPUTATION, both for quality and service? It need not be a household word but it should have a good name in its field, however restricted this may be. Its salespeople should be able to say with pride 'I'm from . . .'.
- is it HONEST? Integrity should permeate the company from CEO to office junior, all of whom must

be honest with both their internal customers and their external ones. A company which encourages dishonesty towards customers will almost certainly deny doing so if its salespeople are caught out. At the same time, you can't expect a company which wants you to be less than honest with your customers to be honest in its dealings with YOU. It could, for example, allow sales managers and senior reps to pre-empt all the genuine leads and customers and leave you with an impressive list of names from the dead letter file.

- is it SALES LED AND CUSTOMER DRIVEN? You can't expect to make sales unless the sales force are the company heroes and everyone in the company knows that their jobs depend on the salespeople's performance. Nor can you expect perfect sales unless your company accepts wholeheartedly that sales involve the complete workforce in an ongoing partnership with the customer.

- does it provide a QUALITY product? Products of APPROPRIATE quality – not necessarily luxury products – are easier to sell than others.

- is it WELL MOTIVATED? Outward and visible signs of this are well-kept exteriors and interiors – including reception areas and toilets – welcoming, helpful receptionists and secretaries. Look also for evidence of mutual respect between grades.

- is it SUCCESSFUL? Success is catching. Selling for a successful company gives its salespeople a tremendous lift. It also implies that the products are intrinsically saleable.

- does the company in question offer FAIR REWARDS to its salesforce? Ideas on this vary but a company offering a salary sufficient to cover your basic outgoings, plus performance-based earnings averaging around twice that figure – with NO UPPER LIMIT – would be about right.

IS THE JOB RIGHT FOR YOU?

Now look at the more subjective factors. Broadly speaking, what would you enjoy selling? What do you think your background, education and experience would enable you to sell well? There's no need to be too restrictive about this – in fact the more flexible you are the better.

List in order of preference the fields in which you feel you would like to be engaged, ranging from 'could bear to sell' to 'could sell with evangelical zeal'.

Would you enjoy a sales position with a multi-national with all the big company benefits, or would you prefer a smaller company where your contribution would per-haps be more appreciated?

Would you like to work for a company which provides opportunities for travel or one which will keep you pretty much close to home?

Should you have to re-locate, how important are items like family, friends or your children's education?

Subjective criteria of this sort affect your 'comfort zone' and have a direct bearing not only on your personal happiness but on your ability to make perfect sales.

Add any other items you consider important and check your current firm or the companies you are considering against the list. Aim for the company that combines the greatest number of positive elements.

FINDING OUT

Once you have a general idea of what constitutes your perfect company, the business section of your local public library, the trade papers and the salespeople's grapevine could provide much of the information you need.

You can learn a lot about the company before the interview stage from a trial phone call and even more from a visit. Try to meet a couple of the salespeople and ask them about conditions and training. If they look and talk like crooks in a TV movie the chances are that the company's idea of a mission statement is 'grab the money and run.'

DON'T SETTLE FOR LESS THAN PERFECTION

When times are hard, especially if you have no specialized background and little or no selling experience, you may have to accept a selling job with a company that is less than perfect. Grab it if it is offered, or hang on to it if you are already in it, but don't SETTLE for it permanently.

Working for a tough, commission–only outfit, for example, could be a genuine learning experience which will help you to hold your own anywhere. It will also keep you while you are looking for the perfect company and the PERFECT PRODUCT.

THE PERFECT PRODUCT

The product is the main link between you and your customer and, if the sale is to be perfect, the product must be perfect – for both parties.

The product is an element of the sale over which you can exercise control by your choice of company.

Obviously you will tend to choose a field which suits you and a company whose products match your background and experience, but you should also make sure that the product or service your chosen company provides is one which you will find saleable. This may seem self-evident, but the world is full of companies determined to inflict their products on people who have little or no need for them and, while a good salesperson is quite capable of selling the Emperor an invisible suit, taking a job with a company which requires you to perform this feat on a day to day basis is not a great career move.

The world also contains a great many salespeople who are out of step with their product. Ensure that you are in step by choosing the type and importance of product you will sell. Would you, for example, prefer to sell:

- Tangibles – eg. office equipment, machinery?
- Intangibles – eg. insurance, educational courses?
- Expensive products?
- Less expensive products?
- Small products in bulk?

BIG IS SOMETIMES BEAUTIFUL
In most cases you will have to sell more of a less expensive product to achieve the same income as for

larger products. With limited selling time at your disposal this could lead to hasty calls and perhaps impose a ceiling on your income.

In many ways it is easier to sell costly items (or products in bulk) than cheaper ones. As a customer, you may have noticed that because the sums of money involved are much greater than those we handle every day, it is sometimes easier to buy a car than a pair of shoes. In the case of more expensive products, you will usually be dealing with people who are used to making professional decisions concerning large amounts of money.

At the moment you may not feel too confident about your ability to sell more expensive products, but this again is something you can control by working on your most valuable asset – YOURSELF.

AVOID THE 'TIRED' PRODUCT
You need to know the product's shelf life. Has it been on the market a long time? If it has become a 'standard', is there a chance it may be superceded? Favour companies with extensive Research and Development programmes, especially those who consult their salespeople to find out what customers really need.

WOULD YOU BUY THE PRODUCT?
Put yourself in the position of the prospective customer. Check the company's advertisements and sales literature for quality and content. How does the product measure up against competing products? Are there a great many competing products?

FEEL THE QUALITY
Examine the product itself. How does it compare in terms of quality and price? What are its advantages and disadvantages?

If there is a range of products, are they well chosen with

the customer in mind; or are they a nightmare hodge-podge of bolt-on improvements, dreamed up by a despairing production department? Would you buy with confidence if the salesperson was able to answer a few specific questions to your satisfaction or would you have to be sold – and sold hard?

IDENTIFY THE 'SIZZLE'

Advice often given to salesmen is to 'sell the sizzle, not the sausage'; in other words to sell what the product can DO for the customer, rather than the product itself.

Look for the sizzle in the products you are selling or are being asked to sell and then go further; look for the mouthwatering appearance and aroma, the extra something which would make the products irresistible.

Don't expect the company responsible for the product to have identified ALL its sizzle elements and ALL the prospects who could find them irresistible. We know of one case, for instance, where a sales manager brought in as a last resort discovered that his demoralized salespeople had no faith in the product because they had been advised to sell to the wrong prospects. Once it was pointed out to them that the product was a mouthwatering proposition when offered to a different set of prospects, sales rocketed.

Naturally the product has to fulfil its promise. It should be a product conceived, designed and realized with specific customers in mind, rather than cobbled together for the convenience of a production department anxious to maximize the use of equipment.

If the customers and their requirements are paramount in the minds of everyone in the organization the chances are that you have found the Perfect Company and the Perfect Product and are well placed to become the PERFECT SALESPERSON.

3

THE PERFECT SALESPERSON

YOU are without doubt your most important re-
source. You are also the factor in the perfect sale over
which you have most control.

You can even decide what you will call yourself. Are
you a salesman – or saleswoman – a salesperson, a sales
representative or a sales counsellor?

'Representative' is too easily shortened to the less
attractive 'rep', while sales counsellor, though an exact
job description for the perfect salesperson, sounds
clumsy and pretentious.

Some successful companies believe that an impressive
title like Regional Sales Adviser helps their people get in
to see prospects. However, no matter what it says on
your business card, we believe that you should think of
yourself as a salesman or saleswoman.

In fact, you can take pride in being a professional salesperson because the word 'sell' is derived from the Latin
word 'conSILium' meaning to counsel, which means
that you are a professional sales counsellor with a role to
be proud of.

A PERFECT ATTITUDE
Pride in yourself and what you do is an important com-
ponent of the perfect selling attitude. Like confidence, it
leads to a high self-esteem which communicates itself to
everyone you meet, from receptionists to CEOs and,
like confidence, it is a factor you can control.

Cultivate a successful attitude by taking care of things
like:

- **PERSONAL APPEARANCE** – self-evident and for this reason perhaps often neglected: badly cut hair, overlong or bitten fingernails, and so on, indicate disrespect for the customer and can lose sales. Get smart!
- **DRESS** – clean and neat, obviously: buy the best you can comfortably afford but dress without ostentation. Shoes are especially important and in addition to their effect on your appearance can add to your comfort and efficiency.

Aim for a style of dress similar to that of most of your prospects. Carry a choice of outfit in the car to help you play the chameleon. Remember your aim is to make the prospect feel comfortable and relaxed.

- **ANNOYING HABITS** – most of us have acquired a few habits which customers may find distracting. Ask your partner, if you have one, to identify these and help control them. If you are a smoker, smoke only if invited to do so by a customer who smokes.
- **PHYSICAL FITNESS** – selling is fun but it can be demanding. If you are not already fit, join a health club or take up a sport. If you are really fat, as opposed to merely plump, lose weight. Being overweight saps energy, ruins posture and has an adverse effect both on your self-image and the way you are perceived by others. Fit people are perceived as more energetic, better organized and more efficient than fat people. Very fat people are regarded as slobs, plump people are seen as easy going and dependable: plump to slender is fine, while anorexic is almost as bad as obese.
- **VOICE** – aim for a pleasing sound. It is important to avoid monotony. Use a tape recorder to check your voice and delivery for the 'sleeping pill' factor. Generally speaking, low-pitched voices are thought of as reliable and authoritative, so avoid squeaks.

- ACCENT – here again, your aim should be to make your prospect feel at ease, which is difficult to do if your accent is completely different from theirs. Don't try to imitate your prospect's accent, unless it happens to be one you grew up with. Merely modify your own accent slightly, to minimize any contrast which can sometimes be perceived as aggressive.
- VOCABULARY – a good vocabulary not only helps you to avoid monotony, but is a useful selling tool in its own right. Increase your vocabulary by wide-ranging reading. Make sure you know all the jargon and buzz words in your field but be sparing in their use.
- HONESTY – is the best way to sell a policy, or anything else for that matter. It is not only an essential ingredient in the perfect sale but also saves you having to remember exactly what you said when you last met the prospect.
- RESILIENCE – if your attitude is good and your self-esteem high you will be more resilient and better able to cope with the occasional rebuff.

THE TRICK WITH CONFIDENCE

Self-confidence is a vital factor in achieving the perfect sale, and one which can be built up.

1. Selling experience itself will give you confidence. If there are prospects you are apprehensive about, remember that they are only human. Try visualizing them in situations which demonstrate their common humanity.
2. Broaden your social horizons. Visit, say, a four-star hotel and a working men's club, your nearest polo ground and an all-in wrestling tournament. Exercise your social muscles in this way and few prospects should hold any terrors for you.
3. Become adaptable. Join your local amateur dramatic society. After playing a role, however small,

in front of a theatre full of people, an audience of one is a breeze.

4. Grab any chance that offers to speak in public, especially on matters relating to your work.

5. Cultivate a lordly approach to life's minor accidents, social gaffes and so on. Most prospects will forgive human error but do not react favourably to signs of nervous embarrassment.

6. Most people have good days and bad days. You can do a lot to minimize the number of bad days by positive thinking and psyching yourself up, but if you have, say, a streaming cold, stay at home and do some admin – otherwise you will feel depressed and your germ-menaced prospects will be in no mood to buy.

To achieve perfect sales, aim for a Win–Win solution. Before you can begin to do this you must be the sort of winner who knows how important it is to win, without making other people lose. (See the *Winners* series by the same authors.)

This means that, before you go anywhere near a prospect, you should feel, as the French say, 'happy in your skin', totally in tune with who you are, what you are doing and what you intend doing in the future.

Re-modelling yourself and your attitude will help you make perfect sales but, if you are to get the maximum benefit from your efforts, you must also be PER-FECTLY ORGANIZED.

4

PERFECT ORGANIZATION

If you are already working for the perfect company, many of your secretarial and managerial chores will be taken care of, but if the company is less than perfect in this respect, administration is a factor which you can almost certainly influence.

No matter what part your company plays – or can be persuaded to play – if you are aiming for perfect sales and thinking in terms of business building, you should consider yourself a Sales Manager with a sales force of one.

To a great extent you are working for yourself and if this shift in emphasis means a change in attitude to things like hours, record keeping and so on, so much the better.

WOULD YOU EMPLOY YOURSELF?

Ask yourself whether or not you are hard-working, reliable, well motivated, well trained and punctilious in your dealings. Are you bringing in plenty of quality business and are you determined to build up your sales figures to the maximum?

Seeing yourself as your own sales manager may change your idea of what constitutes a perfect salesperson.

As your own sales manager you will be happy to keep records of your activities. If the records your company asks for are useful, take photocopies of them for your own files.

THERE'S 'TIME' AND THERE'S 'SELLING TIME'

Don't forget that, in addition to being a manager, you are also an entrepreneur, building up a business in which your main investment, apart from ability and experience, is TIME.

Work out your hourly rate for the time you spend actively selling to prospects. When looked at in this way, it may be frightening to see how much a leisurely cup of coffee can cost you, but resist the temptation to give up coffee: effective self-management will give you more time both for selling and for relaxing.

START WITH MAPS
You need a good road map of your whole area and detailed street maps of all the cities or towns. Keep a duplicate set in the car.

If you have an office in your home, use a large scale wall map you can see while using the phone and 'flag' all prospects and customers. In addition to the obvious information, this will tell you if you are favouring certain areas and neglecting others.

BEGIN THE PERFECT FILING SYSTEM
It's difficult to believe in these days of easily accessed headquarters computers, but there are still companies around whose idea of sales office records is a collection of dog-eared file cards in a couple of old shoe boxes.

Even if your current company does better than this you still need a system of your own. Your livelihood depends on good, up-to-date intelligence, so it is unwise to rely on the information gathered by your predecessors. Like you, they were obliged to provide the company with formal reports on their customers. However they were not obliged to report details like the fact that a particular customer could often be tracked down to the nineteenth hole of his local golf club.

Get the power of the computer behind you
If you can afford it, buy a basic word processor: that way you can add or subtract information when necessary

and print out hard copy of the files you need to have with you for reference.

Open files on COMPANIES, PROSPECTS and CUSTOMERS. Use the headings you are comfortable with and file all the information you have at the moment both on disc and in hard copy files. Note on the computer the presence of any material available only in the appropriate hard copy file, like magazines, newspaper clippings and so on.

Your files should contain all the information you can get hold of about your customers. They should also provide 'management' information about your own performance.

Use the computer, for instance, to keep sales records and to make sales projections. As your own sales manager you can afford to be completely frank with yourself. That way, if any element of your performance is less than perfect, you can improve it.

GO FOR GOLD!
Set yourself targets. Unless your company sales targets are unrealistic, the ones you set yourself should be higher – but they must be achievable.

If you haven't got one already, do get hold of a personal organizer for use with your files, and a notebook – electronic or otherwise – to keep in your briefcase or car. Organize your day, your week, your month and your year in advance. Check how your actual performance in, say, the number of calls made compares with your projection.

Use your records to find out where all your selling time has been going. Then, if you have sales managers or other staff who call head office meetings in selling time, or summon you to lunches which extend well into the afternoon, point out that THEY are losing with every minute you are not in front of a potential customer. With a little tact, even training sessions, seminars and the like can be re-scheduled to fit in with YOUR selling and business-building efforts.

Being your own sales manager means that, as a business builder, you can be totally committed to discovering more prospects, persuading them to become purchasers and turning them into PERFECT CUSTOMERS.

5

THE PERFECT CUSTOMER

At first glance, the customer appears to be one element of the sales process over which you have little or no control. However, you may have more influence on this factor than you think.

Begin with territory, if you have a specific one assigned to you. If you feel you are in a strong position when you first take the job, the 'honeymoon' is the time to discuss territory with your new company. You may find, for example, that you lose territory in the course of a takeover, or that one or two good customers are mysteriously transferred to the books of your more senior colleagues. You should be able to reclaim at least some of what is due to you. If not, wait until you are in a stronger position before asking for an equitable number of perfect and potentially perfect customers.

RATING PROSPECTS

Take a good hard look at your current client list. As a new recruit you may have been introduced to some of them, or have discussed them with your sales manager, but whatever the state of your intelligence files you can now begin listing your customers with reference to their degree of perfection.

Open three files labelled: NEAR PERFECT, AVERAGE and SOBs. Use whatever term you like for the third file but it should express what you think of the companies or individuals concerned.

Skim the cream

Start with the near perfect prospects. Visit these at the beginning of the month and leave the tough customers to the end. If you are taking over a territory, plan to leave yourself time at the end of the month for tackling the SOBs.

Go for the pleasant, easy sales first, and the 'probables' next. They fill quotas and pay packets; they are also a terrific morale booster for when you tackle the SOBs.

HOW TO RECOGNIZE THE PERFECT CUSTOMER
The perfect customer should be:

- easily accessible. If an otherwise perfect customer is way out on the borders of your territory, resist the temptation to have a pleasant trip until you have some sales under your belt.
- demonstrably able to derive benefit from an IM-MEDIATE investment in your product. There is a temptation to go for the pleasant prospect who might just be interested. Leave them till later. Not only will this mean that you are using your time profitably but, if you are less 'hungry', your customer's needs will come first and you will be less likely to oversell.
- a decision maker or, in the case of a large order, someone with direct influence on the decision-making process. 'Selling' to someone who is in no position to buy is a waste of time.
- someone with a budget or direct access to a budget sufficient to buy your product. This is linked with decision making but, especially when making the first contact, try to ensure that the person you are speaking to has budget control. If the firm in question insist that you speak first to a person who is not really empowered or able to buy, put them on the back burner. If they want to employ someone to perform a pre-selection of salespeople they are placing a barrier between you and your potential customer; treat them accordingly.
- someone who knows what you are talking about

and has the authority to call in technical help if needed, once they decide they are interested in what your product can do for the company. It's up to you to keep things simple and to adapt your presentation to suit the prospect, but it's no use trying to sell to a person who doesn't understand what you are saying.

- someone who will make an appointment, see you on time if it is humanly possible and give you a reasonable hearing, while asking a secretary to field and filter any possible interruptions.
- someone who is anxious for any information you can give them which is going to help them identify, quantify and solve their problems.
- a person who could be of active help to you in your business building by providing referrals, endorsements, word of mouth publicity etc.
- a person who with luck will become not merely an ally but a friend.

WHEN EVERY PROSPECT PLEASES

Once you have sorted out your files into Almost Perfect, Average and SOBs, open up another file for new prospects.

The word 'prospecting', with its gold–mining connotations, is a splendid one to describe the activity of seeking out potential customers.

Don't be content with worked out veins and small outcrops. By all means pick up any nuggets that happen to be lying around, but go for the mother lode, perhaps in the shape of a completely new type of client for your product. You could strike a bonanza.

Use day dreaming, word association and lateral and even upside down thinking about your company's products and the needs they might satisfy. Don't rely entirely on your company for new ideas. We know of one firm that went belly up because they were convinced that the only possible customers for their products were people who made tail suits. The dress designers who rushed to buy their stock from the Official Receiver knew better.

List all the possible uses of your company's products – perhaps asking someone to 'brainstorm' with you, so that no possibility, however off-beat, remains unconsidered. Look further into those that still seem remotely feasible the following day, but retain even the weird ones – they could set you off on a completely different tack next time.

Use the Yellow Pages to check for companies who might be able to use your product in new ways. They could become prospects.

CONSTANT PROGRESSION
Think in terms of HUNTING new prospects, TAMING SOBs and FARMING AND BREEDING good customers. Your aim is a constant progression towards perfection, with new prospects entering the system as the others move upwards.

Meanwhile, each activity provides you with a different set of satisfactions, each of which in its own way helps to provide THE PERFECT MOTIVATION.

6

MOTIVATING THE PERFECT SALE

For sheer satisfaction it's hard to beat the spine-tingling thrill of the Perfect Sale and the warm glow salespeople experience when they achieve tangible success and equally tangible reward.

MOTIVATION = MONEY – AND LOTS MORE

MOTIVATION implies movement. In fact everything motivates – or moves – everyone to some degree. In most cases you can easily tell which factors have a negligible effect and those which have real impact.

People's reactions to motivating factors are essentially subjective and things which may seem unimportant to most of us can be highly motivating – or demotivating – to individual customers.

Things can not only move us with varying degrees of intensity but also in different directions. However, it is convenient to think of MOTIVATION as movement in the desired direction and DEMOTIVATION as its opposite. In this way we can think of salespeople and customers alike as being motivated or demotivated by specific factors.

Abraham Maslow's famous 'hierarchy of needs' remains a convenient way of illustrating how people are motivated by a series of a wants.

In the Perfect Sale, while your NEEDS and those of your customer will differ in intensity, the sum of the SATISFACTIONS obtained by both parties should be equal, like two pies of the same size made with different quantities of the same ingredients. For instance, you

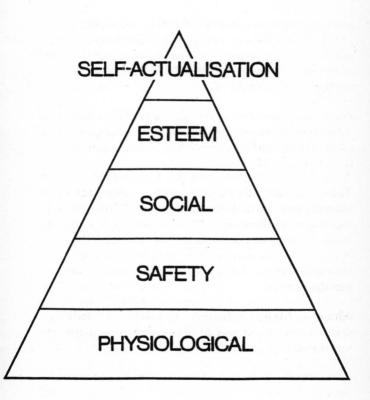

THE ABRAHAM MASLOW
'HIERARCHY OF NEEDS'
PYRAMID

SELF-ACTUALISATION

ESTEEM

SOCIAL

SAFETY

PHYSIOLOGICAL

might place a larger value on physiological needs than your customer, but this is by no means invariably the case, and discovering which needs are most important to individuals and how to balance them is one of the vital steps in the perfect sale.

Once you have discovered what moves or motivates yourself and others, you can control or influence motivation to achieve the perfect sale.

Begin with what motivates YOU as a salesperson. Some of these factors will have been partially taken care of by your company – the better the company the better the motivation – and once again this is something you should be able to influence.

What we are looking at now are the satisfactions YOU can derive from the whole selling process, many of which come under the heading of 'self-motivation'.

THE PERFECTLY MOTIVATED SALESMAN
Looking at the steps on the Maslow Pyramid, and bearing in mind that salespeople are 'Hunters', 'Animal Trainers', 'Farmers' and 'Stockbreeders', you can estimate the importance of satisfying each need:

Physiological
The perfect sale will help satisfy many of your physiological needs since it is by making sales that you feed, clothe and house yourself, and your family if you have one. For most salespeople the satisfaction of this particular category of need (usually in the form of earnings) is both important and immediate.

Safety
Part of the fun of selling is that it is not a safe profession. Like hunting, the selling 'game' is something of a gamble, but as a wise hunter you will do your best to secure

your home and to weigh the odds in your favour. Nowadays most companies enable their salespeople to enjoy the hunt while secure in the knowledge that lack of results – in the short term – will not mean starvation.

Social

Paradoxically most salespeople are gregarious creatures who work alone. Wise companies do their best to make them feel part of the company family, but the fact remains that during the working day the people a salesperson has most to do with are customers. Coffee and business lunches emphasize this social aspect of selling.

Esteem

The perfect sale will earn you the esteem of your company and your customer, but self-esteem derives from the knowledge that you have done the best possible job of counselling.

Self-Actualization

Self-actualization is the process of becoming a complete human being, a genuine winner, happy in one's skin, and is based on character, capacity and talent rather than position or money. Perfect selling, with its ability to contribute to our understanding of ourselves and others, provides many self-actualizing satisfactions.

WHAT MAKES YOU RUN?

List in order of importance the things which motivate you as a salesperson – the needs which you expect to satisfy. You may be surprised to discover that money, while high on your list, is less important than you thought, while social esteem or self-actualizing factors are more so. Getting the mix right for YOU will make it easier for you to realize perfect sales.

Now list the demotivating factors. Do you, for example, find your current selling job stressful and therefore detrimental to your family life and your health? Do you hate your boss, despise your colleagues or loathe your customers? You can control or influence these factors even if, in extreme cases, you have to change your company.

Keep these lists of motivating and demotivating factors. Your aim should be to increase the motivating factors and eliminate the demotivators so that you become a perfectly motivated salesperson, absolutely confident of your ability to turn prospects into PERFECTLY MOTIVATED CUSTOMERS.

7

THE PERFECTLY MOTIVATED CUSTOMER

If we knew exactly what motivated each potential customer, making perfect sales would be easy.

Fortunately we are able to predict what most people's reactions to various motivating factors will be and, at the same time, we can research our individual prospects to discover any idiosyncratic motivations.

Like salespeople, potential customers are influenced in the course of the selling process by a series of needs. Finding out how you can satisfy many of their needs, instead of just one or two, will vastly increase your selling power. These needs include:

Physiological
Here, the need is likely to be less immediate and obvious than in the case of salespeople but, in the long run, making the correct decision could affect your customers' incomes and thus their ability to provide food, clothing etc., for themselves and their families. You are there to help them.

Show them how your product will save money, increase production, avoid waste and generally make their company more profitable. Whatever helps the prosperity of the company will have a beneficial effect on THEIR physiological needs.

Safety
Every good decision that purchasers make strengthens their position and makes them more secure. As the converse is true, you need to provide reassurance. Tell them about your company's excellent record for quality

products and first class service. Remind them of any of their competitors and associates who have successfully used your product.

Social

The customer has the advantage of an office 'comfort zone', a workplace family which provides for many of his social needs like 'stroking' and communication. However, the salesperson, as a new or rarely seen face, can provide additional stroking, new and interesting information and a glimpse of a wider world. In many cases they can also relieve boredom.

See yourself in a social role, a welcome visitor who is not merely a distraction, since you are there to discuss business. Become a sounding board for gossip, gripes and grumbles. This is not only a way of discovering what problems your prospect may have which your product can solve, but a vital part of your wider intelligence–gathering effort.

Esteem

Making successful purchases will contribute to the esteem in which customers are held by their organization and perhaps by the trade. For example, being the first company to try a new product successfully can earn a cachet of distinction.

Self-Actualization

Your customers need to be able to feel good about themselves. Asked in the right way, they will almost certainly help you. They may also want to be a part of something bigger than themselves. Show how your product will help in a 'noble cause', like keeping production staff employed or making their lives easier, more productive or safer.

Potential customers who are buying for themselves,

rather than an organization, will be subject to the same hierarchy of needs as salespeople and their organizational clients, but once again the mix of satisfactions will almost certainly be different. Esteem factors, for instance, might figure highly among the satisfactions sought by car-buyers, while security would almost certainly be an important consideration for someone buying insurance. Remember, for the perfect sale the sum of satisfactions derived by both parties should be the same.

Make a list of factors you consider will motivate your potential customers to buy. How many of these factors can you control or influence?

CUSTOMER MOTIVATING FACTORS include:

- Product will solve problems.
- Price is justifiable and within the prospect's budget.
- Product will increase profits, save money, eliminate waste.
- Product will simplify production.
- Product will add to company's or individual's prestige.
- Product will give prospect advantage over competition.
- Salesperson's appearance inspires confidence.
- Salesperson demonstrates confidence and enthusiasm.
- Salesperson's approach is courteous but friendly.
- Sales folder is well written and well illustrated.
- Salesperson has excellent knowledge of the product and is able to put this over simply and convincingly.

(ADD AS MANY ITEMS AS YOU CAN, NOTING ALL THOSE YOU CAN CONTROL OR INFLUENCE.)

DEMOTIVATING FACTORS include:

- Salesperson is sloppy, unkempt, carelessly dressed.
- Salesperson's car looks like a hen house.
- Salesperson's manner is offhand.
- Salesperson lacks confidence in self, in the company, in the product.
- Salesperson has only superficial product knowledge.
- Sales material is of poor quality.
- Product is of poor quality.
- Price is totally unjustifiable.
- Firm has poor reputation for service.

(ADD AS MANY ITEMS AS YOU CAN, AND ONCE AGAIN MAKE A NOTE OF THE FACTORS YOU ARE ABLE TO CONTROL OR INFLUENCE.)

WHAT'S IN IT FOR THEM?

The aim of the selling exercise is to show your potential customers how the product will benefit THEM.

Throughout your dealings with them, they will be asking, 'What's in it for me?' and the question is perfectly legitimate. We are all of us ego-centred – even saints enjoy being saintly – but this does not necessarily mean that we are egotistic.

TARGETS

Targets are motivating – so find out what your prospects' targets are and how you can help meet them. Helping your customers from first contact and throughout all your dealings will implant motivations so strong that YOU will be the person they turn to whenever they have a problem – or a project.

PROBLEMS

A project usually involves a series of problems, the solving of which is enjoyable and highly motivating.

As a business builder you should think in terms of providing projects for your customers and for this and many other reasons you will need PERFECT RESEARCH.

8

PERFECT RESEARCH

Research and intelligence-gathering is an essential part of the salesperson's job and one which will help you to make the most of your selling time.

As the Army training manuals put it, 'Time spent in reconnaissance is seldom wasted.'

The first targets for this activity are those firms and individuals to whom you are already selling. You probably know a great deal about them already, in which case all you need do is keep your files up to date as details are constantly changing.

RESEARCHING CUSTOMER COMPANIES

What you need to know about companies who are current or potential clients includes:

- What does the company do? Obvious, but they may have more than one use for your product or more than one division that can use it.
- How is the company or organization set up? Who owns it, who runs it? Is it an autonomous company or part of a group? If they are part of a group, what is the group's buying policy?
- What is the company's reputation a) as a producer, b) as a merchandiser?
- What is the company's attitude to its management and workforce?
- Does the company have a mission statement?
- Does the company have, or is it aiming for, any trade distinctions or awards like BS5750, or even 'World Class' status?
- Is the company Quality-conscious? Has it, for example, instituted Total Quality Management?

- What is the company's attitude towards a) the local community, b) the environment?
- Is the company receptive to new ideas? How does it gather, process and reward employee ideas?
- Has the company bought from you in the past? Is it currently buying from your competitor? If so what and at what cost? Is it satisfied with your competitor's product?
- If the company is currently buying from you, how solid is the business? Are they, for example, flirting with a competitor and, if so, why?

Companies are motivated in the same way as individuals and the same Hierarchy of Needs applies, although once again the mix is likely to be different. The company ethic almost certainly permeates the whole of the workforce to some extent, including the individual you are selling to, which makes it essential to know, for example, whether they are motivated primarily by physiological needs or are deeply into self-actualization, in which case they could have, or be looking for, 'a noble cause'.

- Is the company successful and buoyant or failing and miserable?

The above list of questions will help you gauge the motivation of the company in question when faced with a potential sales transaction but you should also find out if they have any idiosyncratic motivation – like loyalty to a long-term supplier.

Sources of Intelligence
Collecting information will eventually become second nature and the best plan is to take note of all the details you can and to make a record later of those you may need.

Sources include:

- Public libraries, especially the Business Department.
- Local newspapers, especially those close to your customer's premises. If you can talk your way into the newspaper 'morgue' or cuttings library, so much the better.
- Trade papers and magazines.
- Local business magazines.
- Any hand-outs and PR and advertising material put out by the company in question, especially house magazines and staff journals.
- Your Sales Manager and your own company's records, including past sales figures.
- Your predecessors. They are worth talking to even if they have been fired, but their information should be evaluated accordingly.
- Rumour and gossip. Always a good source of intelligence but not always a source of good intelligence. Evaluate.
- Competing companies. Again, evaluate information carefully.
- Your contact or contacts in the company.
- The company's customers. A good source of information on the company's morale, its aspirations and its problems, but one to be exploited with care and tact.

You are looking for NEEDS your product can SATISFY and this entails looking for PROBLEMS and possible PROJECTS. You are also looking for anything to help you get in to see your prospect and to win their attention once you are in their office.

RESEARCHING INDIVIDUALS

All the above sources can be used to research individuals within prospect companies. A local newspaper, for example, could tell you of any outside interests they may have; trade papers and their firm's own publications will tell you if they have been in the news recently.

Knowing that they have recently won a golf tournament, been awarded the OBE or received a public pat on the back from their chairman could help you swing a sale. The firm's publications could tell you a lot about your prospect's needs and likely attitudes.

Your predecessors should be able to give you useful information about your prospect's character, likes and dislikes. Take note but do not pre-judge.

Research your prospect's customers, both external and internal, if you can manage to do so discreetly. Their internal customers could tell you a great deal about them and may easily point out needs they are not aware of which can be satisfied by your product.

Once you get in to see your potential customer, they should be your best source of intelligence about themselves and their needs, both present and future, but you will have to LISTEN in order to pick up on vocal clues and WATCH to pick up on body language.

Avoid cloaks, daggers and trenchcoats. Aim for an air of sympathetic interest. You are not a spy but a potential ally looking for ways in which you can help.

There will also be needs which you have identified from other sources of which your prospect may not be aware, and problems which they do not fully appreciate. Fortunately you will be there to provide counsel and guidance and to offer the perfect product to solve their problems and facilitate their projects. First, however, you have to make the PERFECT APPROACH.

9

THE PERFECT APPROACH

Now is the time to call on as many potential customers as possible.

If you make enough calls you are bound to find someone, somewhere, who is waiting anxiously to buy what you have to sell, no matter what you do or say. Of course, this approach would be an incredible waste of leads and prospects, but the principle of making plenty of calls is sound – so why is it that so many salespeople would rather call in sick than call on customers? The answer is that they lack confidence in both themselves and their product. They are beaten before they begin, so they would rather not begin.

By contrast, YOU should be eager to get started. This is when your perfect preparation begins to pay dividends. You are not just a rep making a call on spec, but a highly-motivated, well-informed professional, confident of your ability to counsel your potential customer and to make a perfect sale.

OPENING THE DOOR BY PHONE

The all-important first contact with your potential customer will almost certainly be by phone and although your background knowledge – like knowing who to ask for and their precise position – will help, it is your telephone manner which will do most to gain you an appointment.

Check your telephone skills by tape-recording a few of your phone conversations. Many people, for example, lack conviction when they phone because they see a piece of plastic rather than the person they are talking to. Act into the phone: smile, grin, frown, bite your lip and wave your hand around. Once you get used to making every call a performance you can even ham it up a little. The phone is your ally. Use it!

If your client has a secretary it will be part of their job to filter the boss's phone calls, which means that it is the secretary who will make an appointment or decide whether or not to put you through. Try 'promoting' the person you are speaking to. Treat the secretary as the PA they almost certainly see themselves as being, the buyer as the Purchasing Manager and so on.

Speak distinctly. Assume that the person at the other end of the line is taking a note and slow down for important items. Practise announcing yourself and your company in a way which makes both sound impressive.

Do NOT try to sell on the phone unless you are in telephone sales. 'Can you give me some idea of what it's about?' calls for an answer something like, 'As I said, I'm David Plinge from Selhams. You'll have seen our advertisements so you'll know that we make high-quality plastic widgets. I'd like to get together with Mr Uptight for a few minutes to discuss any problems the old-fashioned widgets may be causing him and how our new widgets could help solve them.'

This ought to get you put through to the boss. Check his name and try for the secretary's name before you speak to him. 'Good morning, Mr Uptight. As I was saying to Miss Granger, my name is David Plinge of Selham's . . . .

TWO QUESTIONS
Once you have made an appointment, make a note to phone the secretary, ostensibly to confirm the meeting but, more importantly, to ask how much time has been allotted to the meeting and how many people will be present.

DON'T try to sell. DON'T agree to send sales literature through the post. DO leap on the idea that they
may like to see the literature: 'I'll be in the area on Mon-
day around midday. I'll drop the brochures in and take
the opportunity to say hello to you.' Call the secretary
later to tell her when you will be calling and try to get
her to free some time with her boss.

Whatever the outcome of your phone call, always keep
the door open for further calls. If possible, make yourself memorable: for instance, if the person you're talking to has an unusually pleasing or interesting name, say
so. You will have made the first step towards changing
your customer's perception of you from a salesman to a
human being.

Keep calling. In most selling situations, but especially
when seeking appointments, POLITE PERSIS-
TENCE PAYS.

Once you have made your appointment re-check your
potential customer against your files. Ask yourself
again what their needs are and what you can do for
them.

When you call, take the information files you need with
you – but not in your briefcase.

Plan your journey to give you plenty of time and, if
possible, stop a little way from your potential customer's premises for a final appraisal of the strength of your
position:

- You are well-groomed and appropriately dressed.
  Check this. If you are arriving in the middle of a
  typhoon leave yourself time to use your customer's
  cloakroom to make yourself presentable.
- You are fit, rested and full of energy.

- You have everything you need including your order book. Check any sales aids you propose using.
- You have researched the company and the person you are going to see and already have a good idea of their needs. Glance at the file if you need to refresh your memory.
- You have done your best to prepare for the perfect sale and are confident of your ability to conclude it. You are not apprehensive and any butterflies you may feel merely mean that the adrenaline is flowing.

Be punctual. Allow a couple of minutes for tidying up and getting the receptionist or secretary on your side. Secretaries may well feel that they are there to keep salespeople out. It is essential that they become allies in your efforts to help their boss and their firm. It may be difficult to achieve this on the first call but aim for it. Make sure that you know the secretary's name and use it once or twice.

Don't 'knock with a wet sponge' as experienced sales managers put it. In other words don't hand over your card and mumble. Tell them who you are and who you represent in a way that shows you are proud of both.

If you have to wait, use the opportunity to make your mark with the receptionist, especially if they are also the switchboard operator. Take any chance you get to collect information for your files, including reading any of the firm's literature you have not already seen, and perhaps arrange to take a copy with you. Check the reception area for any useful information about the person you are going to see. Pictures of classic cars or racing yachts for example could provide clues.

Take the opportunity to confirm with the secretary

exactly how much time has been allocated to your meeting and to identify those who will be present. If you fail to do this you could be in for a shock.

Try not to sit down, even if the receptionist asks you to. Sitting down saps your energy and puts you at a disadvantage if the prospect comes out to greet you. Standing up increases your visibility and makes the receptionist aware of your presence. It also enables you to prowl around, looking at pictures etc.

If you have an appointment for a specific time do NOT wait for ever. If your prospective customer is obviously busy, and if he or she apologizes for keeping you waiting, be patient, but take your leave – pleasantly – rather than become a fixture in the waiting room. Your time is valuable. Make sure your prospect is aware of this, but don't slam the door. You will almost certainly want to come back through it.

In the normal course of events you will be shown in to see the boss on time. Walk tall! You are on your way to the PERFECT FIRST IMPRESSION.

10

THE PERFECT FIRST IMPRESSION

You never get a second chance to make a good first impression.

Fortunately, the factors that create a good impression are largely within your control and some of them, like smartness, personal hygiene and good posture, are universally desirable.

Other factors especially relevant to the first encounter with potential customers include:

- your smile: walk into your prospective customer's office smiling – not grinning or smirking – and you announce your intention to abandon any adversarial role. You are a guest in THEIR comfort zone. It's up to you to make yourself a welcome guest.
- your greeting: always important but never more so that on first contact. Speak clearly as you greet your prospect and announce yourself. Even if the secretary has already announced you, this gives you a second chance to fix your name and company in the prospect's memory as you say, 'That's right, Mr Farnsbarns. I'm Sally Smith from Frisbees – the widget people.'

SURPRISE! SURPRISE!
If you have not managed to find out in advance how many people will be at the meeting, or if the secretary has not been told about a last-minute change, you could be in for a surprise as you walk into your prospect's office expecting to see only one person and find anything up to half a dozen people facing you.

Don't panic. The presence of several people is a good

sign. After all, if your prospect considers your proposition to be worth not only his own consideration but that of others you have almost certainly crossed the first hurdle by arousing INTEREST.

The advantages of selling to a group may not be immediately apparent when you are faced with what looks like a firing squad, or even when your first social moves have transformed them into a jury. A little more work on your part should turn the jury into a panel, the members of which are prepared to consider your proposition objectively before making a decision.

However, you need to achieve a great deal more than that. You need to turn the people facing you into an audience. Work on the fact that they have all shown interest to help you succeed in this. What you are aiming for is the sort of magic which turns a group of theatregoers into an audience, but remember that this sort of synergy or group energy can work both ways and, if it is to help you, it has to be positive.

Fortunately, you can afford to be more of a role player with a group than when faced with an individual. Try being a little more theatrical than usual, using bigger gestures and more emphatic delivery.

Use humour, if it comes naturally, to seek out an ally. When you have found someone who seems to be on your side, don't address them exclusively but let your eyes cover the whole group as you keep returning to your ally. You should also be on the lookout for any 'hidden power'. This is often a person sitting to one side of your apparent prospect and they can usually be identified fairly easily by their air of authority as they put questions and by the deference shown to them by the others. If your ally is the hidden power you are fortunate. If not, you should shift some of your attention to the decision maker, especially as you move to your close.

If you have succeeded, group enthusiasm should carry the day and you have a ready-made close as you ask, 'Now that you have decided to buy a Super Widget and everyone is satisfied with the decision, who's going to sign the order?'

ASSUME INTEREST

No matter how many people you are selling to, the time you move into your prospect's office is the time to make full use of all the money your company has spent on advertising, as you say, 'You'll have seen our advertising for the new Super Widget in the national press – or on TV.' If they haven't, you have at least established your company as one which is substantial enough to advertise. If they *have* seen the advertisement, confirm their interest as you assert, 'I'm glad you were interested in the advertisement. I think you'll be even more interested when you hear all that our product can do for you.'

Factors which can win or lose you a sale in the first few seconds include:

- your handshake: shaking hands is a deep-rooted, meaningful gesture which is an important declaration of intent. Get a few friends of both sexes to give you their frank opinion of your handshake. If you have a handshake like a limp lettuce, or grasp the other person's hand like a wrestler going for a submission hold, change it. If you have clammy hands you could have a fitness problem: try to solve it, even if it means asking medical advice.

Practise your handshake as though your livelihood depended on it. It does! Take the other person's hand firmly but gently and hold it – briefly, without squeezing. If your prospect wants to arm wrestle – don't! You could win the bout and lose the sale.

- eye contact: making eye contact from time to time is fine, but staring people straight in the eye makes them feel uncomfortable. Besides, your eyes should be busy gathering additional information before you get past the greeting stage.

THE TEN-SECOND APPRAISAL

Your prospect's appearance, their smile – if any – and their handshake will already have told you a lot about them. Use the introduction and handshake time, together with the time it takes to sit down, to check out their comfort zone. Are there any additional clues: family photographs, sporting pictures and trophies, press cuttings, diplomas or business awards?

Ties and lapel badges can provide useful information. If you share an interest or have a school, club or regiment in common, your luck is in – but don't try to fake it. Do:

- sit down in the chair they indicate – to begin with.
- accept a cup of coffee if it is offered. You don't have to drink it all, if doing so will cramp your selling style. On the other hand it does enable you to prolong the first-impression time and accentuates the social nature of the encounter.
- comment favourably, but not fulsomely, on any specially attractive feature of the office such as the view.

Do not:

- smoke unless pressed to do so by someone with an ashtray on their desk.
- comment facetiously or otherwise on the political news of the day or any other controversial topic. Leave this sort of thing until you know your prospect better, and even then be careful.
- put down a hot cup on their priceless antique desk.

Up to this point, good manners is all you need. You are in what to all intents and purposes is the other person's home-from-home and should behave accordingly.

At this stage you should sound out your prospect to make doubly sure how much time they have allotted to your meeting. A prospect who appears to have all the time in the world and then rushes off halfway through the presentation is the salesman's nightmare. The social phase can also be a good time to find out, if you don't already know, whether anyone else is involved in the decision.

The initial social phase should be just long enough to set the tone of your meeting, but its reverberations ought to last until you leave your customer's office and even afterwards.

Provided you have done your homework, and made good use of the time you have spent with the customer so far, you should find the transition from social ex-change to business reasonably simple. The change of gear should be as smooth as you can make it, and if your research or observation has indicated a special interest you will usually be able to find a way to use it to facil-itate this shift of emphasis. For example: 'Talking of classic cars – they really went in for quality when they built those, didn't they, and Frisbees still put that sort of quality first. They've been in the widget business for almost a century, you know, and our latest widgets are still made with exactly the same precision old Jonas Frisbee insisted on.' In the process of changing gear, you have managed to mention your firm's name twice, as well as emphasizing that it is a company which has both new products and a long tradition of quality.

If necessary, use this transition stage, after asking per-mission, to move to a more convenient position for your presentation. The physical move will smooth over your shift of emphasis and at the same time make for a slight break in the ritual.

Provided the person seems to be an average or better prospect, it is enough to bear in mind that selling has evolved into a sort of ritual and that an occasional break in the rhythm is needed if both parties are not to become hypnotized. You will perhaps be making roughly the same presentation several times a day and your customer may well be listening to a similar presentation several times a week and know the classic stages of the selling process as well as you do. Use this to make them feel secure by all means but don't let familiarity with the ritual send them to sleep.

SURPRISE – DON'T MESMERIZE!
Don't use a sing-song delivery. Even if you have said the same things a thousand times they still have to sound fresh and exciting. Change the speed of your delivery, vary the pitch of your voice and its volume. Use a tape recorder to develop interesting speech patterns. Your voice is your best way of getting your message across – make the most of it. If you don't find it inhibiting, put a miniature tape recorder in your pocket or handbag during the sale and analyse your performance and the customer's reactions later.

BE AN ACTIVE LISTENER
Don't go to sleep yourself. Everyone whose job it is to listen develops the facility to switch off while showing every sign of rapt attention. In this passive mode you can often manage to pick up on trigger words and pauses which enable you to continue your presentation. Even so, you have NOT been listening, and although this switch-off facility may be useful for political meetings it is useless for the making of perfect sales. Practise active listening!

Active listening means that you will be able to home in on useful clues as to your customer's needs and persuade them to expand on them.

EVERYONE HAS PROBLEMS

Everyone in business has problems of some sort and most of us are only waiting for a sympathetic ear. Problems are not the same as worries and the best way to deal with your prospect's worries is to turn them into problems capable of solution, especially as problem-solving is one of the most important – and enjoyable – functions of management. Your problem is to get your customers to talk about THEIR problems and to get them to focus on those to which your product will provide a solution.

There are several ways of eliciting those problems which are currently preoccupying your prospective customer:

- Your background reading and day-to-day experience will have made you aware of those problems faced by other people in similar positions.
- Your research may have brought to light specific problems connected with your prospect's company or department.
- Your preliminary conversation may have revealed some of your prospect's current problems and confirmed what you have discovered elsewhere.

Once prospects have acknowledged a problem they will begin to ask – even if in a roundabout way – for the information and specialist counsel you can supply. It is up to you to determine when this stage has been reached so that you are able to move on to the PERFECT PRESENTATION.

11

THE PERFECT PRESENTATION

You have now identified your potential customer's problem and together you are moving towards a solution.

At this stage, if you imagine yourself in the position of the potential buyer, you will be able to see how far you have advanced in the INTEREST, INVOLVEMENT, INVESTMENT sequence and how far you still have to go. As a *buyer*, you would probably be quite some way along this sequence if:

- the salesperson who has been shown into your office is personable, confident and well-mannered.

- they seem proud to work for the firm they represent, an old established company, but none the less one which keeps up with the latest technical developments.

- they have identified at least one current problem which their product might help with.

- you are interested to learn more.

In selling, the other person's point of view is what counts. If you have not aroused a minimum of INTEREST at this point do NOT proceed to the next stage. Think of your prospect as a car with a dead or moribund battery. Give them a rest by returning to the social stage for a few seconds – then try again on a slightly different tack. If they still show no spark, they could be a candidate for SOB status, but don't worry, there are ways of jump-starting even them.

For the moment we are considering an average prospect who has been listening actively and could well become a perfect customer, if subjected to the sort of gentle persuasion which will lead to co-operation rather than confrontation.

The word 'persuade' comes from a Latin word meaning to URGE AND ADVISE. Persuasion is the combination of enthusiasm and counsel needed at this stage of the selling process.

Among the persuaders available to salespeople are sales aids like tapes, videos, models and brochures; in fact your company's marketing people may well have begun the job of persuasion. Whatever the position, your most effective persuaders are words.

CHOOSE YOUR WORDS WITH CARE

You will have begun using persuasive words on your first contact with the prospect's secretary, building up a reassuring picture of your company, its products and you – as its representative. Then, in the all-important first few minutes of your meeting, you will have emphasized some words in order to gauge your prospect's reaction, and used others frequently but without special emphasis to induce an almost subliminal effect.

Your research and observation will have indicated some words you should use and others which you should avoid when meeting a specific customer. Using salty language to achieve an all-boys-together matiness, for example, may not go down well with a prospect who is a lay preacher.

For the most part your choice of words will be dictated by the character of the person you are talking to and the impression you wish to give. However, it is useful to remember that words of Germanic origin will make you sound tough, frank and businesslike, while longer and softer Latin and French inspired words will present you as a subtle, intelligent, well-read negotiator. Be prepared to use both and to adjust the mix.

Accentuate the positive

Avoid negative constructions like 'You may not have heard of us' in favour of, say, 'Of course you're already aware of Frisbee's contribution to the widget-making industry.'

A few conditional constructions like 'you may' are permissible but only to prevent any impression of steamrollering. In general, use 'You *will* be able' rather than 'you *could*'.

Use up-beat phrases from the beginning. Scan the papers diligently and you'll find a paragraph that will enable you to say, 'I see the papers say things are improving and I've certainly noticed a more confident attitude among the people I meet.' Of course you have. You carry confidence with you – and leave a little of it behind when you leave!

Your attitude towards your customer, your job, your company, your product and yourself will often influence your choice of vocabulary.

Use your prospect's name correctly, their company's name with respect and your own company's name with near reverence.

A good attitude will mean you automatically use good words like: you, your company, quality, service, excellence, value, saving, economy, profit, long-lasting, useful, safe, traditional values, novel, breakthrough, help, technical assistance, advice.

Conversely, a bad attitude induces bad words like: me, difficulties, expense, complications, untried, experimental, trouble, breakdown.

(Add your own words to both of the above lists.)

Avoid phrases like 'I'm going to be completely honest with you' which imply that you are not always honest and that you may not have been honest with the prospect until this juncture.

Use the magic phrase 'I wonder if you could help me . . .', or 'Perhaps you could help me get this straight. As I understand it, your people have been having some difficulties with . . . .How much of a problem has this been for you?' Note that their PEOPLE have DIFFI-CULTIES. THEY have PROBLEMS which are capable of solution.

Involve to solve

While you have made it plain from the beginning, both by direct statements and by your choice of subliminal vocabulary, that you are concerned with your prospect's problems and ways you can help solve them, you have been moving towards the next phase in which IN-TEREST becomes INVOLVEMENT.

Of course, while it is convenient to refer to stages, or phases, in the selling process, there is rarely such a neat division in real selling situations. For example, you have been planning to involve your potential customer in the sale long before you met him and have done your research with this in mind, but there is usually a point when you can sense the prospect's active involvement and realize that unless you kick their dog they are going to buy.

Sometimes the prospective customer will upset the progression of the sale. Practise handling this situation, with your partner or a friend acting the customer, and work on it until you can answer questions and get back on track without difficulty. Try to avoid saying 'I'll be answering that question later'. Answer the question both immediately AND later. It is obviously one your customer feels is important and their request for information is a sign of their involvement.

Allow yourself one 'I'm glad you asked that question' per sale. It is a splendid response which has now become a cliché.

In a perfect world your prospective customer would say something like, 'I really feel your new Super Widget could be the answer to my prayers. Let's have a look at some of the technical aspects, shall we?' In a less than perfect world YOU have to decide when they are ready for the PERFECT DEMONSTRATION.

12

THE PERFECT DEMONSTRATION

Your prospective customer is now reassured, at ease and showing interest. It is time to unveil THE PRODUCT.

If your particular Super Widget is small enough you may have a sample with you, but in most cases the product will be presented in the form of photographs, brochures, cassette recordings, films and so on.

Whether you have the product in your brief case, or only its image, treat it as you would the Holy Grail. 'Unveil' the product in a way that implies that this is the high spot of your prospect's day. Even if you are selling something intangible, and have nothing to show but a bunch of papers, handle the documents as though they were the Magna Carta at the very least. You could undo everything you have achieved to date just by slapping down your sales literature on your customer's desk like a bundle of old newspapers.

SELL YOUR COMPANY ON SALES AIDS

If you are already working for the perfect company your sales aids will be the best they can provide – and they will have consulted you and your colleagues to find out what would be of most help. However, if your people have put together a hodge podge of old advertising and marketing material, you may be able to persuade them to invest in new sales aids and influence their preparation. Your prospective customers may not be the only people who need to be sold to. Use your persuasive talents on your own company!

Whatever the nature of your sales aids, all documents

must be neat and clean. If there is any chance that typescript or print, for example, could get covered in finger marks, protect it with plastic covers.

ARE YOU SITTING COMFORTABLY?

By this time you will have placed yourself in the most convenient position for you and for your prospect, which will usually be either at their side or directly facing them.

Facing the client is a good position because you can observe their reactions as you go through your material, but it does mean that you have either to be able to read upside down – which is not as difficult as it sounds – or know the material by heart. Another drawback of demonstrating while facing the prospect is the tendency of some people to clutter their desks with photographs, telephones, pot plants, computers and so on, which means you are either talking over a 'wall' or have to do some serious furniture removing. On the whole it is easier to shift to the prospect's side.

Once you begin, do not allow the sequence of your demonstration to be dictated by the arrangement of your sales material. If you are not completely happy with it, get to know it so well that you can shift to different sections and pages at will.

For instance, you may consider that it is wrong to open with your strongest argument. On the other hand, you may favour hinting at your main selling point in a sort of overture, using it as a theme throughout and then ushering it in with a blast of trumpets towards the end.

Of course, there is a chance that the people who designed your sales aids knew exactly what they were doing. Even if this is the case, do not follow the sales aids slavishly. Once you know them well you can break into them with short anecdotes and quotes to back up what appears in text and graphics. As well as hammering home the points made in your sales aids, this gives your demonstration spontaneity. Remember, however, that if you are offering quotes as proof of statements made in the sales aids those statements must be verifiable.

Do NOT let the prospect grab the sales aids from you unless preventing them from doing so would result in a brawl. Do not let them take possession of any documents which need more than five seconds to peruse. However, if they are not already available, prepare or have prepared, where appropriate, some magnificent pictures of your product, accompanied by a minimum of text, which you can let the prospect hold, as handling even reproductions of products helps people to envisage themselves as owners of the real thing.

This adds force to the picture you are painting of life with a new super widget by accentuating the positive, and often by replacing future tenses, even positive ones, with the present. Compare the force of 'With your super widget installed and running, you have all the advantages of advanced widgetry at your command, including our new widget booster, giving you increased production and eliminating the problems you mentioned' with 'If you should decide to buy our super widget, you would have, etc . . .'

HOLD THE JARGON!
Now is the time to lay out, point by point, the advantages of your product. Do not get too technical or use too much jargon – just enough to hint that, should you choose to do so, you could dismantle and re-assemble a widget while wearing boxing gloves and a blindfold. You should know all about what widgets do and also have some idea about how they do it.

Concentrate on the benefits of your company's new technology and, if the prospect has mentioned problems in any area, lean heavily on the aspects of your new widget that will help solve them. You should have been dropping in the occasional 'investment' from the beginning. Use it more often as you begin to approach the close. For example, 'Your investment in the super widget brings you advantages like . . . ':

- the appearance of the product and how great it looks when installed.
- the ease of installation.
- the speed, safety, cleanliness etc., of the product's operation.
- the special features and the advantages of your product. (Don't knock any similar products they may already have. It could have been your prospect who bought them.)
- the ease of servicing the product which represents a saving in time and money.
- the operator-friendliness of your product which means fewer, if any, complaints from the shop floor or office.

DEFUSE THE DREADED ORDER BOOK

At this stage, if you use an order book or contract, you should have it on your prospect's desk. However, it should be enclosed in a neat folder because most order books and contracts look threatening. In fact, the mere sight of them can hypnotize potential customers to the point where they no longer listen to what you are saying.

Keeping your order book in your briefcase is even worse than having it lying naked on the prospect's desk. When you reach for it you are behaving like a bullfighter going in for the kill. By comparison, taking a form out of its folder is not threatening.

Summarize the main points of your persuasive argument in one or two sentences. Finish with a clincher like, 'Did I mention that your investment is totally protected by our money back guarantee?'

By this time your potential customer should be licking his lips at the thought of owning a new super widget. In fact, when you begin the sale, it's a good idea to have this picture in mind as the state you intend to induce.

You are now ready for the close – always provided that you have been using the PERFECT WAY TO HANDLE OBJECTIONS.

13

THE PERFECT WAY TO HANDLE OBJECTIONS

The perfect way to deal with objections is to regard them as the requests for information which they very often are.

In fact, if your approach has been well carried out, there should be no such thing as objections in the dictionary sense of 'expressions of opposition or dislike'. After all, you have gone to great lengths to create an atmosphere free from both, and although objections is a word we are stuck with, reservations is a better way of describing the attitude of most of those prospective customers who do not leap to buy. Reservations lead to questions and you should be glad if your prospects ask them. It proves they are alive, it suggests they are listening and it may well be telling you that they are interested.

'Will it . . . ?' 'Can it . . . ?' 'Do you . . . ?' and so on are not objections. Learn to recognize them as requests for information even if they are disguised as 'I don't think it will . . .' 'I'm sure it won't . . .' or 'You can't tell me that . . .'

You may have already answered some of your prospective customer's questions. Don't worry; the percentage of verbal information which people hear and understand is surprisingly small. Answer your prospect's questions again as though they were new ones.

WELL-FOUNDED RESERVATIONS . . .
Your company and its products may not be perfect and you should be aware of any weaknesses.

In the long run you should be able to ensure that many

of these weaknesses are put right, but in the short term – always provided the good points well outweigh the bad – you can live with them.

... AND HOW TO DEAL WITH THEM

These weaknesses can provoke genuine objections and one way to deal with them is to answer them before they are made, by bringing them into your presentation to support favourable points.

For example, deal with the weaknesses in a throwaway line: 'The technology of our new super widget is way out in front of anything on the market. In fact, in the early days this bold approach gave us one or two minor problems, but of course that's all behind us now and our pioneering enterprise is paying dividends for our customers.'

If you wait for the objection, your response could come out as, 'Yes, you're right. I'm afraid our new super widgets did break down a lot in the early days, but they don't any more.'

Your research into the customer's company may have indicated a line their objections might take. For instance, if the company is not particularly buoyant, they may feel that it would be wrong to spend money, even if they are interested in the product.

Because you know this to be the case, you may be able to emphasize the savings or extra profits your product would provide, and the fact that the modest investment will pay for itself within a short time, while the savings will continue for the lifetime of the product. Once your prospect has agreed that your product would help solve their problem, ask them to say how much they believe it would save or make for them. Use a piece of paper to work it out together. Specific figures mean a great deal more than generalizations. Be prepared with all the figures relating to quantity discounts, credit facilities and so on.

DON'T BE A 'PRICE-A-PHOBE'

In general, objections on price are really requests for information and you will already have dealt with many of them by emphasizing the quality of your product.

You can also flirt with price by implying that, in the words of one advertiser, your product is 're-assuringly expensive'.

Received wisdom maintains that you should not mention price until the end of your presentation and that if the customer asks the price you should stall them with something like, 'I'll be coming to that later'. While it is patently annoying if they insist on knowing what YOU want from THEM, before you have told them everything they can expect from you, it is usually better to answer them immediately and frankly. On the other hand, if your product comes in a dozen different forms, something like, 'Well I can give you a ball park figure but I'm sure you would prefer to know what different types of super widget are on offer' is permissible. However, don't give your prospect the impression that you are *afraid* of your price.

In most cases your customer's job description, if complete, would include 'spending money'. They will not be as concerned with the amount as they are with making sure that laying it out is justified and justifiable.

Perspective shrinks price

Many objections, especially objections on price, can be dealt with by placing your product and the required investment in a wider context than buy/don't buy. Talking about turnover, plant investment, savings and so on situates the transaction as part of the big picture and emphasizes its comparatively low cost. Let the prospect make the inferences. A conclusion prospects draw for themselves is worth twice as much as one you have to point out to them.

THE UNCONVINCED PROSPECT

If your prospect continues to raise objections this may indicate that:

- you have not been sufficiently convincing.
- they have not completely understood your proposition.
- your product does not in fact satisfy their needs.
- you have not given them enough information of the right kind.

None of the above objections should arise if you have done your homework before meeting your prospective customer. Try for some on-the-spot fence-mending.

Objections which are not your fault, and which you may or may not be prepared for, include:

- your prospective customer is already over budget.
- they have just spent huge amounts on installing someone else's product.
- your prospect and the CEO of your competitor company are golfing buddies.

Do your best, but if you feel you are becoming desperate, leave gracefully and put such prospects on the back burner along with the SOBs in a file marked 'CHALLENGES'.

Once you have made your presentation, and clarified any points your prospect may have raised, summarize your presentation, emphasizing that:

- your company has a splendid reputation for quality and service.
- your products are superior to anything similar on the market.
- your product will solve the problems THEY have mentioned.
- your product will yield the benefits THEY THEMSELVES have estimated. (Quote the figures if they have committed themselves.)
- the investment is minimal when compared with the benefits THEY will derive from it. These are not merely financial – important though savings etc. may be – but include for example: improved safety, trouble-free running, better staff relations, a well-motivated workforce and, by implication, well-earned applause from THEIR boss, THEIR colleagues or THEIR shareholders for THEIR splendid buy.

While they are still glowing with anticipated triumph – go for the PERFECT CLOSE.

14
THE PERFECT CLOSE

The Perfect Close is when the customer says, 'That sounds like exactly what I need and the price is reasonable. When can you deliver?'

However, not all closes are quite so simple, and many salespeople find the close so alarming that they stammer and stutter.

If you find closing difficult you may find it easier to think in terms of 'completing the sale' or bringing it to a 'successful conclusion'.

- The logical outcome of your presentation is that your prospect should agree to your proposition and mark their formal assent by signing an order.
- This should happen so smoothly that you are hardly aware of it, so that 'I'll just get the paperwork out of the way' is as much of a close as is needed.
- However, some customers would rather fight alligators than make a decision, in which case you have to ASK for the business. This is by no means as tough as many salespeople believe. After all, the customer knows that you are there to persuade them that your product will satisfy their needs.
- Offering alternatives is a useful way of concluding a sale, provided you can offer a genuine choice. Your prospect can almost certainly spot a classic alternative close a mile away, so instead, get them to indicate their preferences as you go through your presentation. You can then say, 'I gather from what you were saying earlier, that you prefer the Mark III in green. I'm sure we can fix that up for you.' Some sales transactions have a built-in alternative close: 'Will you want the booster attachment?'

- The query close makes a neat assumption: 'Will there be any problems your end about delivery or installation? No? In that case I'll have our people get in touch with you . . . .'
- The premium close is useful if you are genuinely able to offer special rates, favourable delivery or any other *quid pro quo* for an instant decision. On the other hand, if you feel the sale is not firm, save this sort of argument to cope with 'I'll think it over'.
- Do try just plain asking. It saves an awful lot of waltzing around. 'Right Mr Johnson. I know you are happy that the Super Widget will do the job and you've agreed the price is right. So do we have a deal? Fine!'
- The body language close is an asking close reduced to a smiling look of interrogation, with one hand holding a pen and the other steadying an order form as you say, 'Okay?' and go right ahead.

Even the best of potential customers can make presentation difficult – and closing even more so – by leaping in with questions before you are ready. Be ready! Train yourself to field questions, turn them to your advantage and then get back on track.

EARLY CLOSING

Occasionally a question half-way through a presentation like, 'Fine. When can you deliver?' indicates the opportunity for an early close and you may have been advised to defer replying and to go on with your presentation.

In fact, this can make you sound like one of those self-important politicians whose peevish 'Let me finish!' turns debate into monologue, and if you insist on continuing your presentation you could very easily talk yourself out of a sale.

On the other hand, you want your customer to have

ALL the information which will re-inforce their decision. Your best move is to get your impatient customer to sign the order and then go on with a shortened version of your presentation with a slight shift of emphasis, acknowledging the fact that they are now the proud owner of the product.

REFUSALS AT THE LAST FENCE

Sadly some prospective customers will try to ruin your day by saying, 'Thanks – but no thanks', in which case you have to make a quick decision as to whether they are SOBs in disguise or whether you have failed to convince them.

Once you are certain that they have not been having fun at your expense, express slight surprise as you go through those points on which you have already reached agreement and seek confirmation. Ask for the business again, and if they still say no, suggest that there must be other reasons for this and ask if there is any point that needs clarification.

Try the magic formula, 'I wonder if you can help me.' For example, 'I wonder if you could help me, Mrs Jones. I was absolutely convinced when I walked into your office that our product was perfect for your requirements, and everything you have said has added to my conviction, so why exactly is it that you are not prepared to buy at this time?' This should elicit an answer, even if it is only, 'Well, I want to think it over.'

Thinking it over

If the response is a new objection, answer it and go on with the sale. On the other hand, 'I want to think it over' raises several possibilities:

- Your prospect does not have the authority to make the decision. Ideally you should have known this but some people hate admitting that their authority is circumscribed. Tell them you quite understand that they want to consult their technical people or 'bring in someone with a fresh viewpoint'. Suggest that your prospect brings them in while you are available to answer their questions.

- Your prospect has decided against your proposition. They believe that their 'think it over' is letting you down lightly. Why did they decide as they did? Keep plugging; you can't deal with their doubts until you know what they are.

- Your prospect is one of those people who genuinely likes to mull things over before they make a decision and they have a cast-iron rule never to order in the course of a sales presentation.

Imply that you quite understand, and tacitly approve, their mature attitude and add that you are certain that the more they think about it the more convinced they will be that your product is what they need. Pin them down as to how long the mulling process will take. Make a definite date to call – preferably in person – for their decision. Later, write a letter thanking them for seeing you, outlining your proposition and enclosing any relevant sales material.

If you intend making a follow up phone call, agree a date and time for this and make a note in your diary while you are still with the prospect.

- Your prospect is expecting a visit from your competitors and wants to compare your respective products. Great! They really DO need a new widget. A comparison, you assert, can only confirm that yours is better. When is your competitor coming? Fine, you'll call by the day afterwards for a decision. Make a mental note to phone just before your competitor's visit.

Do NOT knock your competitors or their products. 'They're very good. In fact, they keep us on our toes, which is one reason why our product is so advanced and so dependable; it's also one of the reasons why we provide such outstanding service and offer such competitive prices.'

Whether you have written up the order or not, you may have already made the perfect sale. You now have a second chance to make a good impression as you go for THE PERFECT EXIT.

15

THE PERFECT EXIT

For salespeople seeking to perfect their role, the perfect exit is as important as the perfect entrance. It is a second chance to make a good impression.

Once your customer has signed an order they will normally experience a feeling of mild euphoria, followed almost invariably by 'buyer's remorse'. This is not the time for salespeople to pick up their briefcase and run.

DON'T SELL AND RUN!
This is the time to consolidate the sale, minimize any post-purchase doubts and begin business-building.

Your customer must be reassured that they have done the right thing, that your product will in fact help them in the ways they expect, that it is guaranteed, trouble-free and will benefit from an impeccable after-sales service.

Good representatives re-present
This part of the selling process, though short, is virtually a second presentation. It often carries more weight than the first because in the eyes of the customer this new assertion of 'what's in it for them' is no longer tainted by your eagerness to make a sale.

You can now go on to move your sale firmly into the future. Where appropriate, give them the names of the people who run your accounts and service departments, establishing yourself as a member of an organization rather than a lone salesperson.

PERFECT SALES THAT BREED
While your customer is still feeling completely happy
about the order, give them the chance to achieve another and different satisfaction by asking them to help
you by providing you with new contacts.

At this stage, ask for contacts rather than endorsements.
If your customer says they can't give you either until
they have tested the product, make a mental note to
hold them to what is, in effect, a promise.

If they are able to give you some contacts, take the
opportunity to gather as much information as possible
about the people concerned and their requirements.

If the prospect has NOT yet signed an order, ask for
contacts anyway. They could feel guilty about 'wasting
your time', in which case they may give you some leads
to 'make up' for not placing an immediate order.

On the other hand, if they refuse point blank to assist
you, ask why. The prospect's answer could bring to
light some hitherto unrevealed reasons why THEY
didn't place an order.

If they say, for example, 'I'm not going to be responsible for introducing anyone to widgets that burst into
flames all the time' and you can prove that your products are not a fire risk, you stand a chance of getting
not only leads but the original sale.

TURNING PURCHASERS INTO CUSTOMERS
Once your prospect has bought your product, concentrate on making him a genuine customer in the sense
of someone who 'customarily' buys your products.
Emphasize that you will keep an eye on delivery and installation and will look in 'to see how he is getting on'
once he has had a chance to use the product.

By doing this you are reassuring your right to re-enter your customer's comfort zone in order to provide them with help and counsel. The fact that doing so means you will be immediately aware of any further needs they have, which can be satisfied by your product, is a bonus.

DON'T CROW!

Make it plain that, although they may have signed the order in response to your advice and counsel, you do NOT feel that you have *beaten* them. Both parties have satisfied their needs, a deal has been made and a win-win situation established. You are entitled to indicate your pleasure but, even if you have doubled your salary for the month in a matter of minutes, you should avoid any outward signs of elation until you are in your car and on your way. Thank them for their courtesy – and by implication for the order – but in a way which suggests it was the only logical outcome to your meeting. Shake hands and smile as you leave, with a firm promise to return, preferably on a specific date.

If your customer's secretary is in an outer office you should if possible stop by her desk and thank her for arranging the interview. If she asks how things went, tell her, 'I'm sure Mr Brown will want to give you the details himself but it was a very satisfactory meeting.'

Mention that you have arranged to see her boss again on a specific day and make sure she makes a note of the date and time.

Tell her that her boss has mentioned a couple of people you could see and ask her for the correct spelling of their names, their titles and addresses. With luck, you could obtain further useful information about the people concerned and their needs.

Write down the secretary's name and give her another

of your business cards. Getting the secretary on your side in this way means that you have acquired an ally. This is so important that, should it prove impossible to talk to the secretary on your way out, you should telephone her at the first opportunity.

MAKING ALLIES

If there is a receptionist, switchboard operator or doorman, it makes sense to thank them as you leave and to make time for a short chat which will ensure that next time you call or phone you are recognized as a person with access to the boss.

Whether you are talking to the boss, the secretary or the receptionist, your aim should be to make yourself an honorary member of their workplace comfort zone.

Your subsequent visits should become increasingly welcome and motivating EVENTS. One thing which will help you to achieve this is PERFECT RECORD KEEPING.

16

PERFECT RECORDS

Once you have made a sale, received what appears to be a genuine promise of a sale or had your proposition turned down, wait until you are some distance away from your customer's premises and find a quiet spot to think about your presentation and its implications.

As your own 'sales manager', analysing and recording the results of calls should be a challenging exercise rather than an unwelcome chore.

- If you have been able to make a tape recording of your call, play it back, and make a careful note of any promises you have made to your prospect or customer. Bear in mind that to make a promise and not to keep it is worse than not promising anything in the first place.
- Transfer any dates and times to your personal organizer.
- Make sure that you have written down all the names of the people you have met, together with their positions and extension numbers.
- If you have made a sale, analyse your presentation, either from tape or while your memory is still fresh, to determine the impression you made at each stage of the selling process. Note the high spots of IN-TEREST, INVOLVEMENT and INVEST-MENT. What was it that you said which induced these reactions? Was it something specific to them and their needs which you can emphasize when selling to them again, or something more general which you will be able to use when selling to others?
- If your prospect has promised to 'think it over' and you believe that they genuinely wish to do so, did

they give any indication that they did not intend to commit themselves immediately and at what stage in your presentation did they do this? Could you have done anything to persuade them to make up their mind on the spot? Have you done enough to ensure that they WILL consider your proposition, and what plans have you made to help them do so?

- If your prospect has refused outright to consider your proposition, at what stage did they indicate that this would be the case? Did you have a sale and lose it? If so, why? Did you press them hard enough to give their reasons for not buying? If they gave no reasons and no hint of why they refused to buy, what do YOU think their reasons were?

- Note any requests for information that will allow you to maintain contact with the prospect.

When you get back to base, transfer all the information you have obtained to the appropriate file. If your prospect has made a firm order, for example, they can now be shifted to the 'Customer' section of your files.

As a customer they are now entitled to more, not less, attention than as a prospect.

THE ONGOING PROCESS

Up to now, it has been convenient to consider prospecting, gathering information, selling and customer care separately, but in fact they will usually be carried out simultaneously as part of an ongoing process. In other words, while you are prospecting you may also be selling, and while selling you will be gathering all the information you can about possible purchasers, while doing your best to turn current purchasers into customers.

Like a settler moving into new and unexplored territory, you will be looking for areas suitable for exploitation while at the same time taking any chance game that presents itself.

Motivated by a need for security you will also have begun to behave like a farmer, cultivating those aspects of your selling job which promise a safe and growing return.

This offers plenty of the satisfaction we mentioned when considering Maslow's Hierarchy of Needs:

Physiological
Well sold and well tended, your average to near perfect customers should yield sufficient income to ensure that you can provide yourself and your family with food, shelter, warmth and clothing.

Safety
Customer farming of this sort makes for about as much safety as one can expect. It will almost certainly more than fill your company-imposed sales quotas, which means that your job is relatively safe and free from stress.

Social
Turning purchasers into genuine customers and friends means co-opting them into a club of which you are the peripatetic chairman whose arrival is a welcome social event.

FURTHER UP THE PYRAMID
While organizing sales in this way is highly professional and effective, it is a little low on satisfaction when it comes to the 'higher' needs like esteem and self-actualization.

Of course it does go some way towards satisfying these needs and there are plenty of people who are happy just to establish a comfortable and productive sales round.

Perfect Salespeople are less easily satisfied. They need:

- esteem – in the form of titles, promotion, recognition, peer approval and the sense of belonging to an elite, all of which increase self-esteem as well as eliciting the esteem of others.
- self-actualizing satisfactions – like personal growth and development, the acquiring of arts and skills, creativity, ambition, projects, causes.

In short they need their jobs to be fun, they need excitement and an element of risk, they need to be able to behave at times more like hunters than farmers, which means that as salespeople they need to tackle the PERFECT SOBs AND OTHER CHALLENGES.

17

PERFECT SOBS AND OTHER CHALLENGES

Ideally, by calling on the probables among your prospective clients first, and by tending them once they have become purchasers in such a way as to transform them into customers, you will not only have provided yourself with a sound financial base but will have ensured that you have time to tackle the possibles.

These will include:

- prospects of all types who are geographically remote. Take the probables among these first, but by all means go for them. You have earned a few pleasant trips, especially if there is a good chance of pulling in some business and of discovering further prospects on the periphery of your territory.

- SOBs with a reputation for eating salesmen. These may not be genuine SOBs at all but average or better prospects who have reacted to some bad experience with salespeople by condemning the whole profession. One good thing about this type of prospect is that they will almost certainly have been neglected by your competitors. They could even have begun to wonder why so few salespeople have called on them recently and, having almost forgotten the original incident, may be ready to welcome you with open arms and chequebook.

- SOBs who enjoy a battle. These can be scary for inexperienced salespeople but in fact they are not really SOBs at all. They are merely people who get a kick out of arguing and debating and who can be extremely thrustful in presenting their point of view. They DO see your call as a confrontation and it is up to you to defuse this adversarial element and to emphasize the 'game' aspect. Handled properly, such prospects make splendid customers and add spice and fun to the selling profession.

- SOBs with chips on their shoulders and a built-in resistance to selling and salespeople. Nothing is right for such people, who proclaim loudly that they are not interested and go on to knock everyone and everything in sight.

They can be a pest, but many of them can be turned into average prospects and customers if you listen to their complaints actively and sympathetically. It's worth remembering that some of their gripes may be genuine.

- SOBs whose state is not permanent. These include people with career problems, health problems or domestic problems, all of which they attempt to inflict on you rather than on members of their office comfort zone. They could really be waiting for a sympathetic and objective listener – provide them with one!

- The genuine 24-carat SOBs whose only redeeming feature is that they must, every so often, buy something. These are the sort of people who arrange an interview, keep you waiting and then annul the meeting. Again, they may follow your presentation with every sign of interest, only to take pleasure in announcing that they have no intention of ordering. Such people are waiting for you to cringe and grovel. DON'T!

Steer clear of the genuine SOBs except to phone them every now and again to see if they really want anything.

THE WORST POSSIBLE SCENARIO
Use your most difficult and least productive prospects for experimentation, but first get used to establishing a Worst Possible Scenario.

The Worst Possible Scenario technique can be used in all sales situations but it is most useful in those which seem almost hopeless. It entails simply establishing the worst that can happen and is ideal in the first place for banishing groundless apprehension.

Your prospect, no matter how much of a SOB, is unlikely to:

- set the dogs on you.
- have you ejected from his premises by armed thugs.
- physically assault you while screaming with maniacal rage.
- shoot you stone dead.

If they seem capable of doing any of the above, we suggest you cross them off your prospect – and Christmas card – list.

In fact the worst things that are likely to happen are that they:

- speak coldly to you.
- insult your firm and your profession.
- are sarcastic, patronizing or hurtful.
- shout and swear.

One of the WORST things that can happen to you is that they refuse to buy and that is a situation you intend to change if you possibly can.

Having considered the Worst Possible Scenario, which amounts to nothing much worse than a refusal to place an immediate order, you should then imagine the Best Possible Scenario in which the SOB becomes a purchaser who can be turned into a customer.

One way of dealing with below-average prospects is to

try harder – to the point of exaggeration. Do even more homework on your prospect and their company. Emphasize the other factors to a point close to carica-ture. Work on inducing super self-confidence: bone up on your product knowledge, be ultra meticulous about your appearance and walk especially tall. Charm the SOB's secretary; if you are a woman, be complimen-tary about some aspect of her dress or appearance. Be as respectful to your prospect as you can be without syco-phancy and clutch at straws to provide a social contact: 'So you breed killer dogs – how interesting!'

Massage their ego. Emphasize that THEY are import-ant and that you are there to solve THEIR problems.

You can also use less than perfect prospects to try out some PERFECT WAYS TO BREAK THE MOULD.

18

PERFECT WAYS TO BREAK THE MOULD

No sale is ever quite like the examples given in books on selling, in training videos or even in role–playing classes, mainly because prospects will keep asking questions at the wrong time or leaping off on tangents of their own.

With experience, salespeople learn to cope with this and allow their prospective customers to stray before guiding them back onto the track. Even so, in spite of interruptions and digressions, the presentation tends to become a sort of ritual dance in which both parties recognize every step.

For less–experienced salespeople it is convenient and reassuring to have this recognized progression from introduction to post–close. However, keeping to an established pattern for any length of time can lead to stale presentations, intoned rather than spoken, and with guaranteed soporific effects. Vary the speed of your delivery, change pitch and volume and be continually on the look out for fresh and effective phrases.

Of course, because the well–tried techniques work most of the time, you may be tempted to stick to them all the time, in case you lose the chance of making a sale. The answer is to practise on the SOBs.

EXPERIMENT WITH SOBS

With genuine SOBs you have nothing to lose and everything to gain by breaking the mould and trying out experimental techniques you may be able to use later on your better prospects.

No need to wear a red nose – unless of course it is a charity day – but try out attention–grabbing stunts like

having a scale–model Super Widget roll across the prospect's office floor on a toy truck.

Again, you may have been taught that you must on no
account mention the price until the end of your close.
Rubbish! We are breaking the mould here. Besides, no
one was ever prevented from buying a car they wanted,
and could afford, by seeing the price on the windscreen.

THE PRICE IS RIGHT

Try something like, 'I'd like to mention our price
straight away, Mr Robinson. We're not cheap but we
know we give real value for money. I'll just write down
the price and put it there in front of you so that you can
keep it in mind while we're talking.

'After all, we know you are interested in the product,
otherwise you wouldn't have let me take up your valuable time. All I have to do is to justify your intuition that
the Super Widget will solve some of your problems,
and to give you all the information you need about how
the product can help in your particular situation. Then
we can discuss exactly what you need and talk about delivery and installation.

'Please keep the price in mind. I know you'll be im-
pressed by what you get for your money.'

Try incorporating humour – NOT jokes unless the
customer insists on telling them – into your presentation.

Try changes of emphasis. For instance, there is an un-
written convention that requires salespeople to behave
as though they have just dropped by for a chat and to
impart information about the product, until the very
last moment when the mask is dropped to reveal
SOMEBODY WHO WANTS SOMETHING.

In reality, if your prospective clients are the sort of fish to be taken in by a pretty lure until the hooks sinks in, they don't deserve their job.

Try making it clear from the start that you are there to make a deal and that in return for a fair price you have a lot to offer them. Honesty could get you somewhere.

Try candour: 'You've heard of the trouble we had with our prototype Super Widgets when operating at high speed. Well, we've not only solved the problem but we've used our experience to create a Super Widget guaranteed to operate efficiently at twice the speed of anything else on the market.'

Use charm, when selling to someone of the opposite sex. Combined with flattery, it can turn SOBs into pussy cats and, provided you are talking about a genuine attribute or achievement, you can afford to be fulsome.

BE A STAR!

All selling contains an element of acting and all sales-people eventually adopt the role that best suits them, their product and the majority of their prospects and customers. With SOBs you can afford to try out slightly different roles or even go right over the top. After all, you have nothing to lose.

If they snap, snap back – but smile as you do so. Give as good as you get. You could discover that your SOB is a human being after all and one who finds that having someone stand up to them for a change is enough to transform them from a barely possible to a probable.

Give SOBs every chance to reform – and to buy – but don't waste time on them once it stops being fun. You have better things to do.

SELLING AT THE TOP

Once you have filled your quota, go for the tough sales, for example, sales which are complicated because:

- buying your product would involve your prospect, or their company, in major changes and upheavals.
- buying your product is not a one–man decision.
- buying your product is a decision which, for better or for worse, will put the decision–maker squarely into the limelight.

Such sales often mean that salespeople are confronted by highly–placed and powerful individuals. Some sales-people find this alarming. In fact top people often have a great deal of charm. They usually have a good idea of what they want, together with a shrewd notion of how much they will be prepared to pay for it. What they need is concise and accurate information, so either your product knowledge should be impeccable or you should suggest bringing a technical advisor with you.

NOT 'IS IT WORTH IT?' BUT 'IS IT WORTHWHILE?'

Top people in large companies will not be overly con-cerned with price, provided yours is competitive. If you have identified a genuine need, they will be quicker than most to appreciate your arguments that buying your product will help solve their problem. Once they have made a decision on this, their main concern will be whether or not solving the problem is sufficiently im-portant to them to make it worthwhile coping with any hassle involved in buying your product. Would it, for example, entail extra building? Would it mean any interruption in production?

Such prospects can become not only customers but large–scale accounts. Allow for this possibility and work towards it before your first call, as you prepare to

turn sales into perfect sales and perfect sales into PER-
FECT BUSINESS-BUILDING.

PERFECT BUSINESS-BUILDING

The Japanese concept of 'Kaizan', or constant improve-
ment, was designed primarily to help management but
it is equally applicable to salespeople, especially those
who have realized the importance of being their own
sales managers.

Like doctors, scientists or any other professionals, you
need to keep abreast of the latest techniques and the
most recent advances in your field. You also need to
read as much as you can on sales psychology, body language and so on and to attend any courses and seminars
you consider relevant.

Your reward will be the satisfaction you derive from
making the maximum number of perfect sales and from
knowing that you are a master of your chosen profession.

While you need to know what the experts are writing
and saying about sales and selling, you need only retain
and apply those ideas that really inspire you. If you get
only a couple of new ideas or new slants on old ideas
from a book or a seminar, one of them could be the idea
which will boost your career and change your life.

One way of incorporating new ideas into your own
philosophy of selling is to list both your own ideas and
any new ones you hear about that seem important and
relevant. Write them down and use them as the basis of
brain–storming sessions.

SIMPLIFY
Like any other interaction between human beings, selling is an immensely complicated process. However,

while you should be aware of the complexity of the selling encounter, the details make up too much mental baggage for you to carry into your prospect's office.

One way to simplify matters when in the field is to evolve a basic philosophy embracing everything you have learned which seems important to you.

You could, for instance, decide that in order to aim for the perfect sale you will begin by selling WELL, in which case you need to be:

- well-intentioned, ie genuinely concerned about your prospect.
- well-informed.
- well-motivated.
- well-mannered.

Of course, there are thousands of factors which you could include under each of the main headings, and many of them are mentioned in this book, but once you have accepted the requirements of selling WELL as a sort of mission statement everything else will fall into place, without a great deal of conscious effort on your part.

MANNERS MAKETH MONEY

Being well-mannered, for instance, will *dictate* that you are punctual, courteous and that you allow your prospective client to do at least three quarters of the talking.

You don't have to ask yourself: Is it all right to smoke? Should I interrupt? Should I answer a direct question? Good manners will dictate your correct course throughout.

Good manners will also dictate that, once the order has been signed, you will refrain from leaving an inch of tyre tread in your new customer's car park and that you will keep promises, remain in touch and remember to drop your customer a personal note of thanks and appreciation.

Good manners are good business. Your company may have spent thousands of pounds on advertising and marketing, just to get you into the customer's office which, added to your efforts to get the sale, represent a considerable investment. It would be a shame to lose your sale and a possible account for the sake of a stamp or the cost of a phone call.

It takes a lot more effort to win back lost business or re-place it than it does to keep it. Good manners, by in-fluencing your attitude and actions before, during and after the sale, direct the ways in which you go about business 'farming', which in turn is an important part of Perfect Business–Building.

Business-Building is the creation of accounts – firms who accord you privileged salesman status, whose buyers are loyal customers and who, almost certainly due to your efforts, recognize that you have become their partner in supplying the needs of THEIR custom-ers. It is the logical outcome of the Perfect Sale and one to aim at throughout.

Customers whom you have made into elements of your business will not only think of you first, when they need something you can supply, but will be receptive to your suggestions. Because of the partnership you have established, they will also supply you with informa-tion, together with referrals and recommendations which will help you to build your business.

Business–building makes sense, even though your busi-ness may end when you leave your current position, in so far as it provides increased satisfactions – including more income, improved status, larger pensions and so on.

Thinking of yourself as a business–builder makes it easier to appreciate that the time you spend on training, research, intelligence–gathering, planning and so on, is not merely aimed at a one–off sale, however perfect, but is also designed to ensure future satisfaction.

GENERATE IDEAS FOR YOUR CUSTOMER

Situating your business activities, including sales and research, in this broader context, will help you to fol-low through by thinking in terms of projects your customer could develop, using your products. Talking to their production and sales staff might suggest addi-tional uses for your products.

This sort of business-building also helps create the con-fident attitude which boosts sales and puts individual sales situations into perspective.

Most importantly, business-building calls for quality selling in every respect. This emphasizes the profes-sional nature of selling as a vocation and the fact that, just as surgeons have far outstripped their barber shop forerunners and scientists have moved on since the days of alchemists, selling is no longer the province of the fast-talking, back-slapping wide boy but has evolved into a specialist consultative occupation.

As a business-builder whose aim is quality sales, and whose role is that of counsellor and advisor, you will be able to assert with pride that you are a professional salesperson and, secure in the knowledge that the real secret of your profession is to put the customer first, you will be on your way to making THE PERFECT SALE every time.

Hopefully, we have managed to stimulate your IN-TEREST in quality selling to the stage where you wish for active INVOLVEMENT in the pursuit of perfect sales, and we are confident that you will consider the modest INVESTMENT of time and effort worthwhile.

Of course we are confident that this is the case and that we have sold you on the idea of THE PERFECT SALE.

After all, we are salesmen!